Horsespirations

SWEET & SIMPLE TRUTHS FROM OUR EQUINE FRIENDS

Horsespirations

SWEET & SIMPLE TRUTHS FROM OUR EQUINE FRIENDS

WILLOW CREEK PRESS

Published by Willow Creek Press, Inc.
P.O. Box 147, Minocqua, Wisconsin 54548

Printed in China

ONE DAY OR

Day One

YOU DECIDE

KEEP YOUR FACE TO THE

Sunshine

AND YOU CANNOT SEE THE SHADOWS

Bloom
WHERE YOU ARE
Planted

IMAGINATION Will Take YOU EVERYWHERE

FOLLOW YOUR

Passion

AND SUCCESS WILL FOLLOW YOU

DON'T

Stumble

OVER SOMETHING

Behind

YOU

DREAM Bigger THAN YOU CAN Doubt

IT TAKES A

Long Time

TO GROW AN OLD FRIEND

Everything you want is on the Other Side of Fear

Difficult

ROADS LEAD TO

Beautiful

DESTINATIONS

ONLY A LIFE LIVED FOR *Others* IS A LIFE WORTHWHILE

TIME YOU ENJOY

Wasting

IS NOT WASTED TIME

Limits

ARE FOR

Those

WHO NEED THEM

KNOWLEDGE Speaks WISDOM Listens

THE BEST
View
COMES AFTER THE HARDEST
Climb

YOU ARE MORE

Capable

THAN YOU KNOW

A SWEET Friendship REFRESHES THE SOUL

YOU CAN DO

Anything

BUT NOT EVERYTHING

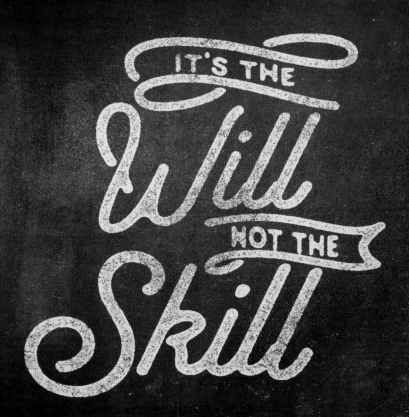

IT'S THE *Will* NOT THE *Skill*

Kindness COSTS Nothing

YOU MIRROR WHAT THE

World

MIRRORS TO YOU

ALONE WE CAN DO SO LITTLE

Together

WE CAN DO SO MUCH

GREET THE

People

YOU LOVE WITH A

Smile

THE
Struggle
IS ONLY PART OF THE
Story

Love FOR All
HATRED FOR NONE

TRY TO BE A *Rainbow* IN SOMEONE'S *Cloud*

BEING Unique IS BETTER THAN BEING Perfect

Obstacles

DO NOT BLOCK THE

Path

THEY ARE THE PATH

ALL THINGS WORK

Together

FOR GOOD

Do Less

WITH MORE

Focus

SOME DAYS YOU JUST HAVE TO

Create

YOUR OWN SUNSHINE

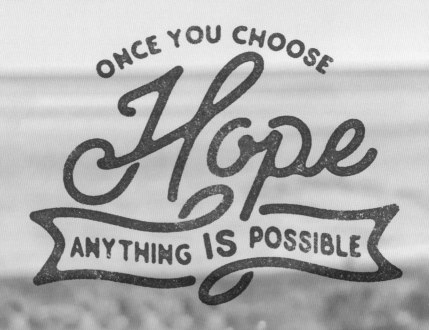

IT TAKES

Strength

TO BE GENTLE AND KIND

WHEN LIFE GETS

Blurry

ADJUST YOUR

Focus

WHEN ONE DOOR

Closes

ANOTHER ONE

Opens

DO NOT
Regret
THE PAST
Learn
FROM IT

Embrace
THE
Journey

Failure is success in Progress

THERE ARE ALWAYS

Flowers

FOR THOSE WHO WANT TO SEE THEM

Sometimes THE ONLY WAY OUT IS Through